Delicious
wraps

Delicious
wraps

Love Food ® is an imprint of Parragon Books Ltd

Parragon
Queen Street House
4 Queen Street
Bath BA1 1HE

Introduction by Frances Eames
Photography by Günter Beer
Food Styling by Stevan Paul

ISBN 978-1-4075-1628-8

Printed in China

Notes for reader
• This book uses metric and imperial measurements. Follow the same units of
measurement throughout; do not mix imperial and metric.
• All spoon measurements are level: teaspoons are assumed to be 5 ml and
tablespoons are assumed to be 15 ml.
• Unless otherwise stated, milk is assumed to be semi-skimmed and eggs are
medium. The times given are an approximate guide only.
• Some recipes contain nuts. If you are allergic to nuts you should avoid using them
and any products containing nuts.
• Recipes using raw or very lightly cooked eggs should be avoided by infants, the
elderly, pregnant women, convalescents and anyone suffering from illness.
• Vegans should be aware that some of the ready-made ingredients in the recipes in
this book may be derived from animal products.
• Vegetarians should be aware that some of the ready-made ingredients in the recipes
in this book may contain meat or meat products.

Contents

Wraps

The wrap is the new take on our old favourite, the sandwich. Wraps are light, bright, fun and healthy – great for packed lunches, light lunches, relaxed outdoor eating or an informal dinner party with friends.

Wraps are big business these days and although they seem to have appeared from nowhere, the wrap has a history of its own. Bobby Valentine, an American former baseball manager, is credited with the invention of the wrap sandwich at his Connecticut restaurant.

Variety

Wraps are one food that will satisfy both healthy eaters and those looking for a guilty pleasure. Whether you're dieting or not, wraps are definitely on the menu. They are easy to prepare and good for the whole family. They take just a few minutes to put together and so are ideal for packed lunches. Variations in tortilla ingredients cater for all needs; for more fibre, substitute whole wheat tortillas for your normal wraps. Or for wheat free recipes, try corn tortillas instead.

Evening entertaining

Wrap and tortilla-based meals are perfect for a casual evening with friends. Mediterranean-inspired recipes are ideal for *al fresco* eating. You can offer several different wraps to accommodate vegetarians and meat-eaters with the minimum of fuss. With an array of fresh ingredients and bright colours, wraps look delicious and take little or no cooking. No wonder they are so popular!

Appetizers and desserts

Wraps are even great to serve as appetizers or desserts. Why not try a modern twist on the traditional appetizers with a Prawn & Avocado Wrap (see page 51)?

For those with a sweet tooth, crêpes and pancakes offer an easy and tasty dessert that can be whipped up in an instant, for example a simple Chocolate & Banana Pancake (see page 83).

Children's favourite

Children love wraps as they can eat them with their fingers. If you are worried about you or your children eating enough vegetables, then wraps are a great way to encourage a wider variety of greens on the menu. Half the fun with wraps is that you can really involve your children in the preparation of ingredients, plus the actual wrapping!

Wrapping – 'the roll'

This is the easiest way. Simply place your filling in the centre of the wrap and spread in a vertical line to the end of the top and bottom sides. Then either fold the left and right sides over the filling, or fold one side over the filling and roll the filled section over the other side. However, be careful not to drop the filling out of the ends of the wrap.

'Open ended'

This way you see the filling at one end but the other end is folded. This method is like creating a pocket. Place your filling in the centre of the tortilla and spread in a vertical line to the end of the top side. Fold the bottom third of the tortilla up over the filing. Take the left and right sides of the tortilla (the part that has no filling on it) and fold it over the filling creating an easy-to-eat pocket.

Don't forget to put out plenty of napkins for sticky fingers!

It's a Wrap!

makes 8

3 tbsp olive oil, plus extra for
drizzling

3 tbsp maple syrup or clear
honey

1 tbsp red wine vinegar

2 garlic cloves, crushed

2 tsp dried oregano

1–2 tsp dried red chilli flakes

4 chicken breasts, skinless
and boneless

2 red peppers, deseeded and
cut into 2.5-cm/1-inch strips

salt and pepper

8 tortillas, warmed

green salad and guacamole,
to serve

chicken fajitas

Place the oil, maple syrup, vinegar, garlic, oregano, chilli flakes
and salt and pepper to taste in a large, shallow dish or bowl and
mix together.

Slice the chicken across the grain into slices 2.5 cm/1 inch thick.
Toss in the marinade until well coated. Cover and leave to chill
in the refrigerator for 2–3 hours, turning occasionally.

Heat a griddle pan until hot. Lift the chicken slices from the
marinade with a slotted spoon, lay on the griddle pan and cook
over medium-high heat for 3–4 minutes on each side, or until
cooked through. Remove the chicken to a warmed serving plate
and keep warm.

Add the peppers to the griddle pan, skin side down, and cook for
2 minutes on each side. Transfer to the serving plate.

Serve immediately with the warmed wraps, a green salad and
guacamole.

makes 4

2 medium-sized chicken breasts

1 tbsp olive oil

2 eggs

4 x 25-cm/10-inch sun-dried tomato wraps

4 baby gem lettuce leaves, washed

4 white anchovies

20 g/3/4 oz freshly grated Parmesan cheese

salt and pepper

for the caesar dressing

3 tbsp mayonnaise

1 tbsp water

1/2 tbsp white wine vinegar

salt and pepper

caesar chicken wraps

Preheat oven to 200°C/400°F/Gas Mark 6.

Place the chicken breasts on a non-stick baking tray; rub with the olive oil and season with salt and pepper. Bake in the oven for 20 minutes. Remove and leave to cool.

Bring a small saucepan of water to the boil, add the eggs, and cook for 9 minutes, then cool under cold running water for 5 minutes. Once cooled, shell and roughly chop the eggs. Shred the chicken and combine with the chopped eggs.

To make the dressing, put the mayonnaise, water, white wine vinegar and salt and pepper to taste in a screw-top jar and shake until blended. Combine with the chicken and egg and set aside.

Preheat a non-stick pan or grill pan until almost smoking, then cook the wraps one at a time on both sides for 10 seconds. This will add some colour and also soften the wraps.

Place a lettuce leaf in the middle of each wrap, roll up then top with the chicken, eggs, anchovies and Parmesan.

makes 4

4 x 25-cm/10-inch wraps

55 g/2 oz cranberry sauce

255 g/9 oz cooked turkey breast, shredded

150 g/5½ oz brie, sliced

salt and pepper

turkey wraps with brie & cranberry

Preheat a non-stick pan or grill pan until almost smoking, then cook the wraps one at a time on both sides for 10 seconds. This will add some colour and also soften the wraps.

Spread the cranberry sauce over the wraps and divide the turkey and brie between the wraps, placing in the middle of each wrap. Sprinkle with salt and pepper and then fold at the ends. Roll up, cut in half on an angle and serve.

makes 8

2 tbsp olive oil, plus extra for oiling

2 large onions, thinly sliced

550 g/1 lb 4 oz lean beef, cut into bite-size pieces

1 tbsp ground cumin

1–2 tsp cayenne pepper, or to taste

1 tsp paprika

8 soft corn tortillas

1 quantity of bottled Taco Sauce, warmed and thinned with a little water if necessary

225 g/8 oz Cheddar cheese, grated

salt and pepper

to serve

avocado, diced

red onion, finely chopped

mustard

beef enchiladas

Preheat the oven to 180°C/350°F/Gas Mark 4. Oil a large, rectangular baking dish.

Heat the oil in a large frying pan over a low heat. Add the onions and cook for 10 minutes, or until soft and golden. Remove with a slotted spoon and reserve.

Increase the heat to high, add the beef and cook, stirring, for 2–3 minutes, or until browned on all sides. Reduce the heat to medium, add the spices and salt and pepper to taste and cook, stirring constantly, for 2 minutes.

Warm each tortilla in a lightly oiled non-stick frying pan for 15 seconds on each side, then dip each, in turn, in the sauce. Top with a little of the beef, onions and grated cheese and roll up.

Place seam side down in the prepared baking dish, top with the remaining sauce and grated cheese and bake in the preheated oven for 30 minutes. Serve with the avocado, red onion and mustard.

makes 4

250 g/9 oz sirloin steak

1 tbsp olive oil

1 tbsp mayonnaise

125 g/4 1/2 oz Stilton cheese, crumbled

4 x 25-cm/10-inch wraps

1/2 small bag watercress

salt and pepper

beef & stilton wraps

Season the steak with salt and pepper.

Preheat a non-stick pan till almost smoking. Add the oil, and then seal the steak, cooking on both sides for 30 seconds. Remove from the pan and set aside for a few minutes. Once the steak has rested, cut into thin strips with a sharp knife.

Mix together the mayonnaise and Stilton cheese.

Preheat a non-stick pan or grill pan until almost smoking, then cook the wraps one at a time on both sides for 10 seconds. This will add some colour and also soften the wraps.

Divide the steak between the wraps, placing along the middle of each wrap. Top with the Stilton and mayonnaise, and then finish with watercress. Roll up, cut in half and serve.

makes 4

2 rump steaks, about
225 g/8 oz each

finely grated rind and
juice of 1 lime

1 fresh green chilli, seeded
and finely chopped

2 garlic cloves, crushed

pinch of sugar

2 tbsp olive oil

1 small onion, thinly sliced

1 red pepper, thinly sliced

4 wheat tortillas

salt and pepper

tomato salsa and soured
cream, to serve

steak & lime tortillas

Thinly slice the steaks. To make the marinade, put the lime rind and juice, chilli, garlic, sugar, and salt and pepper to taste into a large, shallow, non-metallic dish and mix together. Add the steak and turn in the marinade to coat it. Cover and let marinate in the refrigerator for 3–4 hours, turning occasionally.

Heat the oil in a large frying pan over medium heat. Add the onion and red pepper and cook, stirring frequently, for 5 minutes until softened. Using a slotted spoon, remove the steak from the marinade, add to the frying pan, and cook, stirring constantly, for 2–3 minutes until browned. Add the marinade, bring to the boil, and toss together.

Meanwhile, warm the tortillas according to the instructions on the package. Divide the steak mixture among the tortillas, then fold in one side and roll up each tortilla to form an open-ended pocket. Serve hot with tomato salsa and soured cream to spoon on top.

makes 4

½ duck

85 g/3 oz rhubarb

1 tbsp water

2 tsp white sugar

4 x 25-cm/10-inch multigrain
wraps

1 mango, peeled and sliced

4 spring onions, cut into
5 cm/2 inch pieces

small bunch of coriander

salt and pepper

crispy duck wraps with mango & rhubarb

Preheat oven 220°C/425°F/Gas Mark 7.

Place the duck in the oven on a non-stick baking tray and cook for 20–25 minutes or until crispy. Remove from the oven and leave in a warm place to cool.

In a small pan heat the rhubarb with 1 tbsp of water and the sugar, and cook for about 5 minutes or until the rhubarb starts to soften. Remove the pan from the heat and leave to cool.

Pull all the meat off the duck and shred.

Preheat a non-stick pan or grill pan until almost smoking, then cook the wraps one at a time on both sides for 10 seconds. This will add some colour and also soften the wraps.

Divide the duck, mango and spring onions between the wraps, placing along the middle of each wrap. Sprinkle with salt and pepper, top with a spoonful of rhubarb and coriander and then roll up, cut in half on an angle and serve.

makes 4

310 g/11 oz lamb leg steak

$^1/_2$ tbsp olive oil

4 x 25-cm/10-inch wraps

100 g /3$^1/_2$ oz canned piquillo peppers, drained and sliced

55 g/2 oz stoned green olives

small bunch of fresh flat-leaf parsley

salt and pepper

for the aïoli

3 tbsp mayonnaise

1 tbsp extra virgin olive oil

1 clove garlic, crushed

salt and pepper

lamb wraps with peppers & aïoli

Rub the lamb with olive oil, salt and pepper.

Preheat a grill pan until almost smoking. Cook the lamb for 2–3 minutes on each side. The lamb should be pink in the middle. Remove and set aside in a warm place.

To make the aïoli, mix together the mayonnaise, olive oil and garlic and season with salt and pepper.

Slice the lamb into thin strips.

Preheat a non-stick pan or grill pan until almost smoking, then cook the wraps one at a time on both sides for 10 seconds. This will add some colour and also soften the wraps.

Divide the lamb between the wraps, placing along the middle.

Top with peppers, olives and parsley and spoon over the aïoli. Roll up and serve.

makes 4

2 tsp mustard

55 g/2 oz chunky apple sauce

4 x 25-cm/10-inch wraps

280 g/10 oz roast pork, shredded

100 g/3½ oz mature Cheddar cheese, sliced

salt and pepper

roast pork wraps with apple & cheddar

Mix together the mustard and apple sauce and season with salt and pepper.

Preheat a non-stick pan or grill pan until almost smoking, then cook the wraps one at a time on both sides for 10 seconds. This will add some colour and also soften the wraps.

Divide the roast pork and Cheddar cheese between the wraps, placing in the middle of each wrap. Top with the mustard and apple sauce mixture and then fold at the ends. Roll up, cut in half and serve.

makes 20

115 g/4 oz firm tofu

3 tbsp vegetable or groundnut oil

1 tsp finely chopped garlic

55 g/2 oz lean pork, shredded

115 g/4 oz raw prawns, peeled and deveined

1/2 small carrot, cut into matchsticks

55 g/2 oz fresh or canned bamboo shoots, rinsed and shredded (if using fresh shoots, boil in water first for 30 minutes)

115 g/4 oz cabbage, very finely sliced

55 g/2 oz mangetout, julienned

1-egg omelette, shredded

1 tsp salt

1 tsp light soy sauce

1 tsp Shaoxing rice wine

pinch of white pepper

20 soft spring roll wrappers

chilli bean sauce, to serve

soft-wrapped pork & prawn rolls

Slice the tofu into thin slices horizontally and fry in 1 tablespoon of the oil until it turns golden brown. Cut into thin strips and set aside.

In a preheated wok or deep pan, heat the remaining oil and stir-fry the garlic until fragrant. Add the pork and stir for about 1 minute, then add the prawns and stir for a further minute. One by one, stirring well after each, add the carrot, bamboo shoots, cabbage, mangetout, tofu and, finally, the egg pieces. Season with the salt, light soy sauce, Shaoxing rice wine and pepper. Stir for a further minute, then turn into a serving dish.

To assemble each roll, smear a pancake with a little chilli bean sauce and place a heaped teaspoon of the filling towards the bottom of the circle. Roll up the bottom edge to secure the filling, turn in the sides, and continue to roll up gently.

Fisherman's Catch

makes 4

310 g/11 oz fresh salmon fillet

1 tbsp olive oil

4 eggs

2 tbsp mayonnaise

2 tbsp soured cream

20 g/³/4 oz capers, chopped

zest of 1 lemon

chopped fresh dill

4 x 25-cm/10-inch wraps

salt and pepper

salmon & dill wraps

Preheat oven 200°C/400°F/Gas Mark 6.

Place the salmon on a non-stick baking tray, brush with olive oil and season with salt and pepper. Cook in the oven for 8–10 minutes. Remove and leave to cool.

Bring a small saucepan of water to the boil, add the eggs, and cook for 9 minutes, then cool under cold running water for 5 minutes. Once cooled, shell and roughly chop the eggs.

Flake the salmon into a bowl, removing the skin if there is any. Add the eggs, mayonnaise, soured cream, capers, lemon zest and dill.

Preheat a non-stick pan or grill pan until almost smoking, then cook the wraps one at a time on both sides for 10 seconds. This will add some colour and also soften the wraps.

Divide the salmon mixture between the wraps, placing in the middle of each wrap. Then fold at the ends, roll up, cut in half and serve.

makes 4

4 eggs

2 tbsp water

3 spring onions, finely chopped

small handful of fresh coriander, finely chopped

1 tbsp groundnut or vegetable oil

soy sauce, to serve

for the filling

1 tbsp groundnut or vegetable oil

3 spring onions, roughly chopped

225 g/8 oz raw squid, cleaned and cut into chunks if large or rings if small

115 g/4 oz raw prawns, peeled and deveined

115 g/4 oz skinned white fish fillet, such as cod or coley, cut into 2.5-cm/1-inch cubes

1 head pak choi, roughly chopped

1 tbsp green curry paste

1 tsp Thai fish sauce

spicy thai parcels

Preheat the oven to 190°C/375°F/Gas Mark 5. For the omelettes, beat the eggs, water, spring onions and half the coriander together in a bowl. Heat 1 tablespoon of oil in a 20-cm/8-inch non-stick frying pan. Drizzle a quarter of the egg mixture over the base of the frying pan to make a rough lacy pattern. Cook over a medium-high heat for 2 minutes, or until just set, then use a palette knife to turn the omelette over and cook on the other side for 1 minute. Slide out onto a plate or chopping board. Repeat with the remaining mixture to make 3 more omelettes and add to the plate or board.

For the filling, heat 1 tablespoon of oil in the frying pan, add the spring onions and all the seafood and cook over a medium heat, stirring frequently, for 2–3 minutes until the squid is firm, the prawns have turned pink and the fish is just cooked through. Transfer to a food processor and process for 30 seconds, or until just mixed. Add the pak choi, the remaining coriander, the curry paste and fish sauce and process again to a coarse mixture.

Arrange the omelettes on a chopping board and put a quarter of the seafood mixture in the centre of each. Roll one side of each omelette over the filling, fold in the adjacent 'sides' to cover the filling, then fold up the omelette to make a small, square parcel. Transfer the parcels to a baking sheet.

Bake in the preheated oven for 10–15 minutes until lightly browned and heated through. Serve immediately with soy sauce.

makes 24

cooked king prawns, peeled
and tails left intact

2 tbsp sweet chilli dipping
sauce

24 wonton wrappers

groundnut or vegetable oil,
for deep-frying

for the dipping sauce

1 tbsp sesame oil

3 tbsp soy sauce

1-cm/½-inch piece fresh
root ginger, peeled and finely
chopped

1 spring onion, finely
chopped

prawn wraps

Toss the prawns in the chilli sauce in a bowl. Remove the
wrappers from the packet, but keep them in a pile and covered
with clingfilm to prevent them drying out. Lay one wrapper on
a work surface in front of you and brush the edges with water.
Place a prawn diagonally across the square and fold the wrapper
around the prawn to enclose it, leaving the tail extended. Repeat
with the remaining wrappers and prawns.

Heat the oil in a wok or a deep saucepan or deep-fat fryer
to 180–190°C/350–375°F, or until a cube of bread browns in
30 seconds. Add the wraps, in batches, and cook for
45 seconds–1 minute until crisp and golden all over. Remove
with a slotted spoon, drain on kitchen paper and keep warm
while you cook the remaining wraps.

Meanwhile, to make the dipping sauce, mix the sesame oil, soy
sauce, ginger and spring onion together in a bowl. Serve in small
serving bowls with the wraps.

makes 4

4 x 25-cm/10-inch wraps

200 g/7 oz cooked crayfish tails

1 mango, peeled and sliced

½ cucumber, deseeded and quartered

small bunch of fresh mint

small bunch of fresh coriander

for the dressing

2 tbsp yogurt

1 tbsp mayonnaise

1 tsp medium curry paste

1 tsp mango chutney

salt and pepper

crayfish wraps with mango & cucumber

To make the dressing, mix all of the ingredients together.

Preheat a non-stick pan or grill pan until almost smoking, then cook the wraps one at a time on both sides for 10 seconds. This will add some colour and also soften the wraps.

Divide the crayfish between the wraps, placing them in the middle of each wrap, and then top with mango, cucumber, mint and coriander.

Spoon over the dressing, then fold the wraps in at the ends, roll up, cut into slices and serve.

makes 4

200 g/7 oz tinned tuna,
drained

4 tbsp mayonnaise

70 g/2½ oz pitted green
olives, chopped

4 spring onions, sliced

small bunch of fresh
flat-leaf parsley, shredded

4 lettuce leaves, washed

4 x 25-cm/10-inch wraps

salt and pepper

tuna mayonnaise wraps with olives

Mix together the tuna, mayonnaise, olives, spring onions and parsley in a bowl, then season with salt and pepper.

Preheat a non-stick pan or grill pan until almost smoking, then cook the wraps one at a time on both sides for 10 seconds. This will add some colour and also soften the wraps.

Place a lettuce leaf in the middle of each wrap, then divide the tuna mixture between the wraps, placing on top of the lettuce leaf. Fold at the ends, roll up, cut into slices and serve.

makes 4

250 g/9 oz baby fennel

150 g/5½ oz fresh or canned
white crab meat

4 tbsp mayonnaise

zest and juice of 1 lemon

small bunch of fresh
flat-leaf parsley, shredded

4 x 25-cm/10-inch
Mediterranean herb wraps

salt and pepper

crab & fennel wraps

Cut the fennel in half lengthways and then slice thinly.

Place the sliced fennel in a bowl with the crab meat, mayonnaise,
salt and pepper, lemon zest and juice and the parsley. Mix well.

Leave for 5 minutes to allow the lemon juice to wilt the fennel
slightly.

Preheat a non-stick pan or grill pan until almost smoking, then
cook the wraps one at a time on both sides for 10 seconds. This
will add some colour and also soften the wraps.

Give the filling mixture another stir and then divide between the
wraps, placing in the middle of each wrap. Then fold at the ends,
roll up, cut in half on an angle and serve.

makes 8

about 450 g/1 lb firm-fleshed
white fish, such as red
snapper or cod

¼ tsp ground cumin

pinch of dried oregano

4 garlic cloves, very finely
chopped

150 ml/5 fl oz fish stock

juice of ½ lemon or lime

8 flour tortillas

2–3 romaine lettuce leaves,
shredded

2 ripe tomatoes, diced

salt and pepper

salsa, to serve

lemon halves, to garnish

fish burritos

Season the fish to taste with salt and pepper, then place in a pan with the cumin, oregano, garlic, and enough stock to cover.

Bring to the boil, then cook for 1 minute. Remove the pan from the heat. Let the fish cool in the cooking liquid for 30 minutes.

Remove the fish from the liquid with a slotted spoon and break up into bite-sized pieces. Place in a non-metallic bowl, sprinkle with the lemon juice, and set aside.

Heat the tortillas, one at a time, in a non-stick pan, sprinkling them with a few drops of water as they heat. Wrap the tortillas in foil or a clean tea towel to keep them warm while you heat up the rest.

Arrange the shredded lettuce in the middle of one tortilla, spoon on a few big chunks of the fish, then sprinkle with the tomatoes and roll up. Add some salsa and repeat with the other tortillas. Serve immediately garnished with lemon halves.

makes 4

½ cucumber

200 g/7 oz smoked mackerel, flaked

200 g/7 oz cream cheese

½ red onion, finely chopped

1 tbsp horseradish

zest of 1 lemon

chopped fresh dill

pepper

4 x 25-cm/10-inch wraps

smoked mackerel wraps with horseradish

Cut the cucumber in half scrape out the seeds with a spoon and then cut into small dice.

Place the cucumber, mackerel, cream cheese, onion and horseradish in a bowl and mix well. Once combined add the lemon zest, dill and pepper. You will not need salt, as the mackerel is salty enough.

Preheat a non-stick pan or grill pan until almost smoking, then cook the wraps one at a time on both sides for 10 seconds. This will add some colour and also soften the wraps.

Divide the mackerel mix between the wraps, spreading the mix evenly over the wrap. Fold in half and then again and again. You should end up with a cone-shaped wrap.

makes 4

310 g/11 oz fresh tuna steak

1 tbsp olive oil

½ tsp cracked black pepper

½ tsp cumin seeds

4 x 25-cm/10-inch sun-dried
tomato wraps

salt

for the tabbouli

20 g/¾ oz couscous

1 tbsp extra virgin olive oil

1 tomato, chopped

1 spring onion, finely
chopped

small bunch of fresh
flat-leaf parsley, shredded

salt and pepper

tuna & tabbouli wraps

Rub the tuna in the olive oil, and sprinkle with the cracked black pepper, cumin and salt.

Heat a non-stick grill pan until almost smoking then grill the tuna for 30 seconds on both sides. Remove from the pan and set aside. If you prefer your tuna more cooked through, cook it for another 30 seconds each side.

To make the tabbouli, put the couscous and olive oil in a heat-proof bowl, pour on enough hot water to just cover the couscous and leave for 5 minutes.

After 5 minutes stir the couscous with a fork to separate the grains. If the couscous is still a little hard add more water and repeat the process.

Add the tomato, spring onion and parsley to the couscous and season with salt and pepper to taste.

Preheat a non-stick pan or grill pan until almost smoking, then cook the wraps one at a time on both sides for 10 seconds. This will add some colour and also soften the wraps.

Divide the tabbouli between the wraps and top with the tuna pieces, then fold at the ends, roll up and serve.

makes 4

1 ripe avocado

200 g/7 oz cooked peeled
prawns

4 x 25-cm/10-inch wraps

4 baby gem lettuce leaves

for the dressing

3 tbsp mayonnaise

1 tbsp tomato ketchup

1 tsp Worcestershire sauce

dash of Tabasco

salt and pepper

prawn & avocado wraps

Cut the avocado in half, remove the skin and cut into 8 pieces.

To make the dressing, mix the mayonnaise, tomato ketchup, Worcestershire sauce and Tabasco, together in a bowl. Season with salt and pepper, add the prawns and mix again.

Preheat a non-stick pan or grill pan until almost smoking, then cook the wraps one at a time on both sides for 10 seconds. This will add some colour and also soften the wraps.

Place a lettuce leaf in the middle of each wrap and divide the prawn mixture between the wraps. Top with avocado, and then fold in at the ends. Roll up, cut in half and serve.

Fresh from the Garden

makes 8

30 g/1 oz unsalted butter

¹/₂ tbsp sunflower oil

200 g/7 oz leeks, halved, rinsed and finely shredded

salt and pepper

freshly grated nutmeg, to taste

1 tbsp finely snipped fresh chives

8 savoury crêpes

85 g/3 oz soft goat's cheese, rind removed if necessary, chopped

leek & goat's cheese crêpes

Melt the butter with the oil in a heavy-based saucepan with a lid over a medium-high heat. Add the leeks and stir around so that they are well coated. Stir in salt and pepper to taste, but remember the cheese might be salty. Add a few gratings of nutmeg, then cover the leeks with a sheet of wet greaseproof paper and put the lid on the saucepan. Reduce the heat to very low and leave the leeks to sweat for 5–7 minutes until very tender, but not brown. Stir in the chives, then taste and adjust the seasoning if necessary.

Place 1 crêpe on the work surface and put one-eighth of the leeks on the crêpe, top with one-eighth of the cheese, then fold the crêpe into a square parcel or simply roll it around the filling. Place the stuffed crêpe on a baking tray, then continue to fill and fold or roll the remaining crêpes.

Should you wish to serve the crêpes hot, preheat the oven to 200°C/400°F/Gas Mark 6. Place the crêpes on a baking tray in the oven and bake for 5 minutes, or until the crêpes are hot and the cheese starts to melt.

makes 4

1 red onion, cut into eighths

1 red pepper, cored and cut into eighths

1 small aubergine, cut into eighths

1 courgette, cut into eighths

4 tbsp extra virgin olive oil

1 clove of garlic, crushed

100 g/3¹/₂ oz feta cheese, crumbled

small bunch of fresh mint, shredded

4 x 25-cm/10-inch sun-dried tomato wraps

salt and pepper

roasted vegetable & feta cheese wraps

Preheat the oven to 220°C/425°F/Gas Mark 7.

Mix all of the vegetables, olive oil, garlic, salt and pepper together and place in the oven in a non-stick oven tray. Roast for 15–20 minutes or until golden and cooked through.

Remove from the oven and leave to cool. Once cool, mix in the feta and mint.

Preheat a non-stick pan or grill pan until almost smoking, then cook the wraps one at a time on both sides for 10 seconds. This will add some colour and also soften the wraps.

Divide the vegetable and feta mixture between the wraps, placing along the middle of each wrap, roll up, cut in half and serve.

serves 4

2 tbsp olive oil

1 large onion, finely chopped

225 g/8 oz button mushrooms, finely sliced

2 fresh mild green chillies, seeded and finely chopped

2 garlic gloves, crushed

250 g/9 oz spinach leaves, torn into pieces if large

175 g/6 oz Cheddar cheese grated

8 flour tortillas

vegetable oil, for deep-frying

spinach & mushroom chimichangas

Heat the oil in a large, heavy based frying pan. Add the onion and cook over a medium heat for 5 minutes, or until softened.

Add the mushrooms, chillies and garlic and cook for 5 minutes, or until the mushrooms are lightly browned. Add the spinach and cook, stirring, for 1–2 minutes, or until just wilted. Add the cheese and stir until just melted.

Spoon an equal quantity of the mixture into the centre of each tortilla. Fold in 2 opposite sides of each tortilla to cover the filling, then roll up to enclose it completely.

Heat the oil for deep-frying in a deep-fryer or large, deep saucepan to 180–190°C/350–375°F, or until a cube of bread browns in 30 seconds. Deep-fry the chimichangas 2 at a time, turning once, for 5–6 minutes, or until crisp and golden. Drain on kitchen paper before serving.

makes 4

4 x 25-cm/10-inch wraps

4 cherry tomatoes, halved

1/2 cucumber, deseeded and quartered

55 g/2 oz baby spinach leaves

for the hummus

200 g/7 oz canned chickpeas, drained

1 clove garlic, crushed

4 tbsp extra virgin olive oil

1 tsp tahini

1 tsp lemon juice

55 g/2 oz stoned green olives, chopped

small bunch of flat-leaf parsley, shredded

salt and pepper

green olive hummus wraps

To make the hummus place the chickpeas, garlic, olive oil, tahini and lemon juice in a food processor and blend until smooth. Season with salt and pepper. Scrape into a bowl and mix in the olives and parsley.

Preheat a non-stick pan or grill pan until almost smoking, then cook the wraps one at a time on both sides for 10 seconds. This will add some colour and also soften the wraps.

Spread the hummus over the wraps and divide the cherry tomatoes, cucumber and spinach between them, placing in the middle of each wrap. Fold at the ends, roll up, cut in half and serve.

makes 4

100 g/3¹/2 oz green beans, trimmed

100 g/3¹/2 oz canned borlotti beans, drained

100 g/3¹/2 oz canned kidney beans, drained

¹/2 red onion, finely sliced

4 tbsp extra virgin olive oil

1 tsp red wine vinegar

100 g/3¹/2 oz cooked beetroot

1 ripe avocado

4 x 25-cm/10-inch herb wraps

salt and pepper

three-bean wraps

Blanch the green beans in salted, boiling water for 30 seconds and then run under a cold tap until cold. Drain and reserve.

Place the borlotti beans, kidney beans, red onion, olive oil and red wine vinegar in a bowl, add the green beans and season with salt and pepper.

Meanwhile cut the beetroot into 2.5 cm/1 inch dice and cut the avocado in half and remove the stone. Peel and roughly chop, before adding to the bean mixture with the diced beetroot. Mix well.

Preheat a non-stick pan or grill pan until almost smoking, then cook the wraps one at a time on both sides for 10 seconds. This will add some colour and also soften the wraps.

Divide the filling between the wraps, placing in the middle of each wrap, and then fold at the ends. Roll up, cut in half and serve.

makes 4

280 g/10 oz mature Cheddar
cheese, grated

140 g/5 oz chunky vegetable
piccalilli

4 spring onions, chopped

salt and pepper

4 x 25-cm/10-inch wraps

cheddar & piccalilli wraps

Mix all the ingredients together and season with salt and pepper.

Preheat a non-stick pan or grill pan until almost smoking, then cook the wraps one at a time on both sides for 10 seconds. This will add some colour and also soften the wraps.

Divide the mixture between the wraps, placing in the middle of each wrap, and then fold at the ends. Roll up, cut in half and serve.

makes 4

280 g/10 oz cooked beetroot, diced

100 g/3¹/₂ oz Roquefort cheese, crumbled

100 g/3¹/₂ oz walnuts, halved

1 tbsp mayonnaise

55 g/2 oz rocket

4 x 25-cm/10-inch multigrain wraps

pepper

beet & roquefort wraps

Mix the beetroot, Roquefort, walnuts, and mayonnaise together. Season with pepper to taste and gently add the rocket leaves.

Preheat a non-stick pan or grill pan until almost smoking, then cook the wraps one at a time on both sides for 10 seconds. This will add some colour and also soften the wraps.

Divide the mixture between the wraps, placing in the middle of each wrap, and then fold at the ends. Roll up, cut in half and serve.

makes 4

3 red onions, cut into eighths

3 tbsp extra virgin olive oil

250 g/9 oz goat's cheese crumbled

100 g/3$^{1}/_{2}$ oz toasted flaked almonds

1–2 tbsp shredded fresh flat-leaf parsley

4 x 25-cm/10-inch wraps

salt and pepper

goat's cheese & caramelized onion wraps

Preheat the oven to 220°C/425°F/Gas Mark 7.

Mix the onions and olive oil together, and season with salt and pepper. Place in a non-stick oven tray, and cook in the oven for 15–20 minutes until golden and cooked through.

Remove from the oven and leave to cool.

Combine the onion mixture with the goat's cheese, almonds and parsley and set aside.

Preheat a non-stick pan or grill pan until almost smoking, then cook the wraps one at a time on both sides for 10 seconds. This will add some colour and also soften the wraps.

Divide the filling between the wraps, spreading the mix evenly over the wrap. Fold in half and then again and again. You should end up with a nice cone shape wrap. Serve immediately.

makes 4

200 g/7 oz new potatoes,
halved

4 eggs

55 g/2 oz watercress

4 tbsp mayonnaise

1 tsp mustard

1 small white onion,
finely chopped

4 x 25-cm/10-inch wraps

salt and pepper

egg & watercress wraps

Put the new potatoes in a small pan and cover with water, add a small amount of salt. Bring to the boil and then simmer for 15 minutes or until cooked. Drain and once cool, chop the potatoes into bite-size pieces.

Bring a small saucepan of water to the boil, add the eggs, and cook for 9 minutes, then cool under running water for 5 minutes. Once cooled, shell and reserve.

Roughly chop the watercress and eggs and then place in a bowl with the potatoes, mayonnaise, mustard and onion. Season with salt and pepper, then mix until all the ingredients are well combined.

Preheat a non-stick pan or grill pan until almost smoking, then cook the wraps one at a time on both sides for 10 seconds. This will add some colour and also soften the wraps.

Divide the mix between the wraps, placing in the middle of each wrap, and then fold at the ends. Roll up, cut in half and serve.

makes 4

4 x 25-cm/10-inch wraps

3 fresh buffalo mozzarella
cheeses, drained and sliced

4 plum tomatoes, each one
cut into eighths

55 g/2 oz rocket

for the pesto

70 g/2¹/2 oz pine nuts

1 clove garlic, crushed

1 small bunch basil

4 tbsp extra virgin olive oil

70 g/2¹/2 oz Parmesan cheese,
freshly grated

salt and pepper

mozzarella & pesto wraps

To make the pesto put the pine nuts, garlic and basil in a food processor, then blend adding the olive oil a tablespoon at a time. When the mixture is smooth, scrape into a bowl, and add the Parmesan cheese and the salt and pepper.

Preheat a non-stick pan or grill pan until almost smoking, then cook the wraps one at a time on both sides for 10 seconds. This will add some colour and also soften the wraps.

Spread the pesto over the wraps

Divide the slices of mozzarella between the wraps. Place in the middle of each wrap, top with the plum tomatoes and rocket. Fold at the ends. Roll up, then cut into slices and serve.

4

All Things Sweet

makes 8–10

115 g/4 oz plain flour

25 g/1 oz cocoa powder

pinch of salt

1 egg

25 g/1 oz caster sugar

350 ml/12 fl oz milk

50 g/1¾ oz butter

icing sugar, for dusting

ice cream or pouring cream,
to serve

for the berry compote

150 g/5½ oz fresh
blackberries

150 g/5½ oz fresh blueberries

225 g/8 oz fresh raspberries

55 g/2 oz caster sugar

juice of ½ lemon

½ tsp mixed spice (optional)

chocolate crêpes with berry compote

Preheat the oven to 140°C/275°F/Gas Mark 1. Sift the flour, cocoa powder and salt together into a large bowl and make a well in the centre.

Beat the egg, sugar and half the milk together in a separate bowl, then pour into the dry ingredients. Beat together, until a smooth batter is formed. Gradually beat in the remaining milk. Pour the batter into a jug.

Heat an 18-cm/7-inch non-stick frying pan over a medium heat and add 1 teaspoon of the butter.

When the butter has melted, pour in enough batter to cover the bottom, then swirl it around the pan so that you have a thin layer. Cook for 30 seconds and then lift the crêpe to check it is cooked. Loosen the edges of the crêpe, then flip it over. Cook on the other side until the base is golden brown.

Transfer the crêpe to a warmed plate and keep warm in the preheated oven while you cook the remaining batter, adding the remaining butter to the frying pan as necessary. Make a stack of the crêpes with baking paper in between each one.

To make the compote, pick over the berries and put in a saucepan with the sugar, lemon juice and mixed spice, if using. Cook over a low heat until the sugar has dissolved and the berries are warmed through. Do not overcook.

Put a crêpe on a warmed serving plate and spoon some of the compote on to the centre. Either roll or fold the crêpe and dust with icing sugar. Repeat with the remaining crêpes. Serve with ice cream or pouring cream.

makes 8

8 sweet crêpes made with
the finely grated rind of
1 lemon added to the batter

2 tbsp brandy

for the orange sauce

55 g/2 oz caster sugar

1 tbsp water

finely grated rind of 1 large
orange

125 ml/4 fl oz freshly
squeezed orange juice

55 g/2 oz unsalted butter,
diced

1 tbsp Cointreau, Grand
Marnier or other orange-
flavoured liqueur

crêpes suzette

To make the Orange Sauce, place the sugar in a wide sauté or
frying pan over a medium heat and stir in the water. Continue
stirring until the sugar dissolves, then increase the heat to high
and leave the syrup to bubble for 1–2 minutes until it just begins
to turn golden brown.

Stir in the orange rind and juice, then add the butter and
continue stirring until it melts. Stir in the orange-flavoured
liqueur.

Lay one of the crêpes flat in the sauté pan and spoon the sauce
over. Using a fork and the spoon, fold the crêpe into quarters
and push to the side of the pan. Add the next crêpe to the pan
and repeat. Continue until all the crêpes are coated with the
sauce and folded. Remove the pan from the heat.

Warm the brandy in a ladle or small saucepan, ignite and pour it
over the crêpes to flambé, shaking the sauté pan.

When the flames die down, serve the crêpes with the sauce
spooned over.

makes 4

1 large mango, peeled and cut into large pieces

1 small pineapple, peeled cored and cut into large chunks

4 tbsp Greek yogurt

1 tbsp honey

4 x 25-cm/10-inch plain wraps

4 tbsp honey

1 tbsp butter, melted

1 tsp allspice

sweet & spicy wraps

Preheat the grill to high.

Mix together the mango, pineapple, yogurt and honey.

Brush the wraps with honey, sprinkle with allspice and place under the grill for 1 minute. This will add some colour and soften the wraps.

Divide the fruit mixture between the wraps, placing down the middle. Roll up and serve.

makes 8

3 large bananas

6 tbsp orange juice

grated rind of 1 orange

2 tbsp orange- or banana-
flavoured liqueur

for the hot chocolate sauce

1 tbsp cocoa powder

2 tsp cornflour

3 tbsp milk

40 g/1½ oz plain chocolate,
broken into pieces

1 tbsp butter

175 g/6 oz golden syrup

¼ tsp vanilla essence

for the pancakes

115 g/4 oz plain flour

1 tbsp cocoa powder

1 egg

1 tsp sunflower oil

300 ml/10 fl oz milk

oil, for frying

chocolate & banana pancakes

Peel and slice the bananas and arrange them in a dish with the orange juice and rind and the liqueur. Set aside.

To make the sauce, mix the cocoa and cornflour in a bowl, then stir in the milk. Put the chocolate in a saucepan with the butter and golden syrup. Heat gently, stirring until well blended. Add the cocoa mixture and bring to the boil over gentle heat, stirring. Simmer for 1 minute, then remove from the heat and stir in the vanilla essence.

To make the pancakes, sift the flour and cocoa into a mixing bowl and make a well in the centre. Add the egg and oil. Gradually whisk in the milk to form a smooth batter. Heat a little oil in a heavy-based frying pan and pour off any excess. Pour in a little batter and tilt the frying pan to coat the base. Cook over medium heat until the underside is browned. Flip over and cook the other side. Slide the pancake out of the frying pan and keep warm. Repeat until all the batter has been used.

To serve, reheat the chocolate sauce for 1–2 minutes. Fill the pancakes with the bananas and fold in half or into triangles. Pour over a little chocolate sauce and serve.

makes 8

for the pancakes

150 g/5½ oz plain flour

pinch of salt

1 egg

1 egg yolk

300 ml/10 fl oz coconut milk

4 tsp vegetable oil,
plus extra for frying

for the filling

1 banana

1 papaya

juice of 1 lime

2 passion fruit

1 mango, peeled, stoned and
sliced

4 lychees, stoned and halved

1–2 tbsp honey

flowers or fresh mint sprigs,
to decorate

exotic fruit pancakes

Sift the flour and salt into a bowl. Make a well in the centre and add the egg, egg yolk and a little of the coconut milk. Gradually draw the flour into the egg mixture, beating well and gradually adding the remaining coconut milk to form a smooth batter. Stir in the oil. Cover and chill for 30 minutes.

Peel and slice the banana and place in a bowl. Peel and slice the papaya, discarding the seeds. Add to the banana with the lime juice and mix well. Cut the passion fruit in half and scoop out the flesh and seeds into the fruit bowl. Stir in the mango, lychees and honey.

Heat a little oil in a 15-cm/6-inch frying pan. Pour in just enough of the batter to cover the base of the frying pan and tilt so that it spreads thinly and evenly. Cook until the pancake is just set and the underside is lightly browned, turn and briefly cook the other side. Remove from the frying pan and keep warm. Repeat with the remaining batter to make a total of 8 pancakes.

To serve, place a little of the prepared fruit filling along the centre of each pancake and then roll it into a cone shape. Lay on warmed serving plates, decorate with flowers or mint sprigs and serve.

makes 8

325 g/11¹/2 oz ricotta cheese

175 ml/6 fl oz milk

4 eggs, separated

125 g/4¹/2 oz flour

1 tsp baking powder

pinch of salt

55 g/2 oz milk chocolate, grated

2 tbsp butter

for the toffee orange sauce

4 tbsp unsalted butter

85 g/3 oz soft light brown sugar

150 ml/5 fl oz double cream

2–3 tbsp orange juice or Cointreau

chocolate pancakes

To make the toffee orange sauce, melt the butter with the sugar in a saucepan over low heat until the sugar has melted, stir in the cream and bring to the boil. Simmer for 3–4 minutes. Remove from the heat and stir in the orange juice or Cointreau. Set aside.

To make the pancakes, put the ricotta cheese, milk and egg yolks in a mixing bowl and stir well. Sift in the flour, baking powder and salt, add the chocolate and mix well.

Whisk the egg whites until stiff, then fold into the ricotta mixture.

Heat a non-stick frying pan and wipe with a little of the butter. Spoon in 2 tablespoons of the batter and cook for 2–3 minutes, until bubbles appear, then flip the pancake over and cook for an additional 2–3 minutes. Repeat with a little more butter each time until you have 8 pancakes. Serve topped with the sauce.

makes 4

300 g/10½ oz apples, peeled
and cored

55 g/2oz sultanas

2 tbsp soft brown sugar

1 tsp cinnamon

4 x sheets filo

4 tbsp butter, melted

icing sugar, for dusting

warm filo wraps
with spiced apples

Preheat oven 200°C/400°C/Gas Mark 6. Cut the apples into
2.5-cm/1-inch size pieces, mix with the sultanas, sugar and
cinnamon.

Lay the filo sheets out and brush with melted butter. Fold each
one in half and brush once more with butter.

Divide the apple mixture between the filo sheets, placing in the
middle of one end. Fold over each side and roll into a cylinder
shape. Brush with butter and sprinkle with icing sugar.

Place in the oven on a non-stick baking tray for 10 minutes or
until golden.

Divide between 4 warm plates and serve.

makes 4

½ tbsp vegetable oil

55 g/2 oz blanched almonds

15 g/½ oz pistachios

150 g/5 oz honey

100 g/3½ oz stale
breadcrumbs

zest of ½ orange

4 x round sheets Asian rice
paper

rice paper wraps with pistachios & almonds

Heat the oil in a frying pan and fry the almonds until they start to colour then add the pistachios. Remove from the pan when the nuts are golden.

Heat the honey in a saucepan over a low heat; add the nuts, breadcrumbs and the orange zest.

Stir continually for 5 minutes until mix has thickened to a paste. Remove from heat and leave to cool.

Place the rice papers on a flat surface and brush with warm water, they will soften and become pliable after a few minutes.

Divide the nut mixture between the rice papers, placing in the middle in a cylinder shape. Fold over ends, roll up carefully and serve.

makes 4

100 g/3½ oz dried figs,
chopped

100 g/3½ oz dried dates,
chopped

15 g/½ oz stem ginger in
syrup, chopped

20 g/¾ oz ginger syrup

200 g/7 oz sushi rice

1¼ cups water

1 tbsp rice vinegar

1 tbsp sugar

sweet sushi wraps

In a large bowl, mix together the dried figs and dates, the stem ginger and the ginger syrup. Leave to infuse for 10 minutes.

Wash the rice in a sieve under a cold running tap until the water runs clear.

Add the water to the rice in a non-stick heavy-based saucepan, bring to the boil and then turn down the heat to low, cook with a lid on until all of the water has disappeared. This will take about 6 minutes. Remove from the heat and leave to sit for 15 minutes.

Stir the vinegar and sugar into the rice.

Place a sushi mat on a flat surface and cover with a layer of cling film.

Using wet fingers, place half of the rice on the mat, spreading it out evenly, until it covers the mat.

Place half of the filling along the centre of the rice.

Lift up the edge of the matt closest to you, and slowly roll away from you in a smooth movement until you have formed a cylinder shape, applying gentle pressure to keep it neat and compact.

Repeat the process with the remaining rice and filling.

Cut off the ends and cut in half and serve.

makes 4

200 g/7 oz dried apricots

150 g/5½ oz rhubarb, roughly chopped

½ pint/300 ml water

70 g/2½ oz sugar

icing sugar, for dusting

whipped cream, to serve

for the calzone

225 g/8 oz plain flour, plus extra for dusting

½ tsp salt

½ tsp easy-blend dried yeast

90 ml/3 fl oz milk

50 ml/2 fl oz tepid water

1 tsp olive oil, plus extra for brushing

sweet filled calzone with apricots & rhubarb

Place the dried apricots, rhubarb, water and sugar in a heavy-based saucepan and stew over a low heat for 15–20 minuets. Remove and leave to cool.

To make the calzone, sift the flour and salt into a bowl; add the yeast, milk and water. Mix with your hands until well combined, turn out onto a floured surface and knead for 5 minutes or until silky. Using your fingers, make indentations in the dough and pour over the olive oil. Mix thoroughly until all of the oil has been absorbed.

Shape the dough into a ball and place in a clean bowl, brush with oil, then cover with cling film. Leave at room temperature for 1–1½ hours or until the mixture has doubled in size.

Preheat the oven to its highest setting, then place a heavy non-stick baking sheet inside.

Divide the dough into 4 on a floured surface and roll into thin pancakes. Divide the filling between the calzone, placing in the middle. Brush with water and fold over, pinching at the edges. Dust with icing sugar. Remove the tray from the oven, carefully place on the calzone and bake for 8–10 minutes or, until golden. Serve with whipping cream.